## Foreword

We are passionate about recognising individual perspectives and amplifying often unheard voices. Throughout Pride Month, Black History Month, and other events, in 2022, informal sessions on creating poetry, prose, and short stories were open to all.

Participants were supported to explore the themes of inclusion and diversity (identity, inclusion, challenges, this is me, allyship, acceptance, and community), and invited to write on any topic they chose to. This anthology brings together these writings, exploring and celebrating diverse voices from across our organisation.

Inspiring, funny and very palpably human these collected works represent the diversity of our workforce. They showcase our organisation's mix of minds, providing a platform for diverse voices and different forms of writing. The pages contain a wonderful mix of strength and fragility.

There is a colourful array of colleagues, friends, family, animals, and natural phenomena. From the snorty-laugh-inducing 'Bean Sandwich', to the evocative and impactful 'Flexibility', the poems prompt readers to consider difference of experience. They shine with individuality as well as reflecting a sense of togetherness. Readers are presented with a compelling invitation to explore diversity in all its forms.

We thank everyone who contributed to the anthology, including the visual artists, who have allowed their work to be used throughout. And special thanks go to Jay for the positivity, creativity and energy she put into bringing our diverse contributors together and producing this rich and eclectic publication. We hope the voices, words and stories it contains help to start conversations, and encourage exploration of different perspectives and experiences, across our organisation and beyond.

Gaven & Kate

## Introduction

Welcome to Diverse Voices 2022. We hope you love this book and it, perhaps, starts a conversation. Thank you to everyone who pulled together to contribute, to get it off the ground, and to drive it through from a crazy idea to a tangible representation of our community in 2022. Many people who contributed to this book had never written poetry or prose before, and each workshop was a joy to see people express and share their unique perspectives. We hope it shines through. Thanks are due in particular to Laura, Liz, Ellie, Kate, Gaven, Rachel, Claire, Jamie, Ana, and so many others who gave their time and energy behind the scenes, to this project. You are fabulous.

Jay

# CONTENTS

# IDENTITY

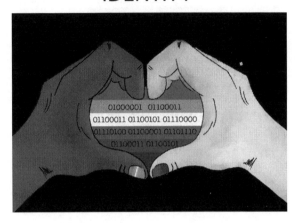

# Identity

Identity is...

What makes me me.

What makes you you.

It is the core,

Of who I am.

Of how I see myself.

Something I wish I was

More comfortable with.

Identity is every facet

Of my being, my hobbies,

Interests and personality.

I may never fully know.

We can never fully see

The picture of

the whole moon, you see.

**Collective Poem**

# Welshman's Wood

Saw you the stag in Welshman's Wood?
I did, he passed by near me.
Saw you the crown around his neck?
I did, I saw it clearly.

And did you hear the Temple bells?
As at the altar table.
The ringing horn above the wood,
The clanging from the stable?

Met you the archers on the hill?
I did, they hailed me kindly.
The hounds and handler in the combe?
I left them far behind me.

Did you tell anywhere he hides
The King among the holly?
My friend I must confess I lied
And sent them to Bourne's Folly.

Alone I rode the downs between
The farms and bone-heaped barrows,
The sheep pens and the hollow barns
Across the ridge and furrow.

From Blackoat Hill to Beechy Bank.
Smallthorns to Toad Corner,
Slate Pits through to Dirty Bridge,
Wind's Hart to Horsepasture.

And then I met the Bourton Road
With weekend traffic streaming
To factory outlet, tea-shoppe, pub
And ended my day's dreaming.

**Mat**

## Identity is...

Identity is

       the sum of attributes

       and characteristics

       that persist

       regardless of

       circumstances

       you find yourself in.

Identity is

       that which is left

       still standing

       when everything

       about you

       is stripped away.

**Jaskartar**

## She

Who is she? So many identities.

Each gives new-found strength:

each a cheerleader when others falter.

The mum, on time for school

despite the flat bike tyre (nailed it!!)

inspires the leader overwhelmed

by her to-do list. The confident work presenter

motivates the nervous Beaver leader,

unsure how to engage buzzing children.

So many identities,

supporting each other,

making me,

me.

**Fliss**

**Everyone**

You                                                              Them




                              We




Us                                                                Me


                    *connect them up*


                        **Anon**

## Lost

I am strong,

I will not be broken

I am fragile,

I break easily and regularly

I am certain,

I know what I stand for,

my hopes, my needs,

I am unsure,

I feel lost and confused.

**Rosie**

# Picture

I am here, I was and I will be.

I am sister, daughter, family, friend.

I am unconventional and unashamed.

I am a jigsaw of a thousand, million pieces,

a picture not yet complete.

**Liz**

## Faster

The sky
   cannot catch
   lightning,
nor the plains
   the cheetah,
nor gravity
   the rocket ship.
I move faster
   than the bonds
   that try to
   grasp me.

**Jamie**

## Off To Have A Baby

Off to have a baby,
Into the deep unknown,
The little one will fill a gap,
And make your house a home.

A miracle being,
Made of two halves,
Sure, to take your lives,
Down new exciting paths.

They don't come with a manual,
Or instructions per se,
A new challenge thrown at you,
each and every day.

I cannot lie,
There will be a mess,
Just try your hardest,
And do not stress.

A massive change,
For your furry babies too,
Not at all sure,
Of this something new.

Night feeds and nappies,

Aren't that bad,

Though sometimes you'll think,

That you have gone mad.

Hold on for that first smile,

It's so worth the wait,

Then you'll remember why,

You got yourself into this state.

But enough from me,

It's been fun,

Time to say goodbye,

Cos you'll soon be a mum.

**Ellie**

## Tightly

I am given purpose;

without it I am untethered,

adrift, unsure away from shore

I am wrapped up in this part of myself;

it binds me like a tight hug, a rope,

it keeps me here but holds me too tightly.

**Rosie**

## Mountain

Shortest of my family,
space for me is certain.

Any taller and I lose my place
in the arms of them,

Enrobed in their love,
I hold the heart of our togetherness close.

Shielded by them,
shielded for us.

My space and place
more certain than a mountain.

**Liz**

# Storm

I am the storm,
   destruction of a hungry crop.
I am afraid,
   hiding beneath the farmyard stock.

I am rage,
I am brave,
I wear the masquerade.

I am always on parade;
I am always afraid.

**Anonymous**

# I Can Never

I can never be a young boy
And live my life that way

I can never relate to how it was
To have a teen romance
Unable to consider dating as a girl

I can never recover years
Spent surrounded by young girls
With barely a boy in sight

I can never experience that strange, flirty way
That young cis boys interact with each other
Only how they treated a girl

I can never make the most
Of canoeing and adventure training
Inaccessible due to dysphoria

I can never learn the ways

That men interact

Not by being as immersed as I should've


I can never gain the prior knowledge

I needed before graduating to young man


**Anonymous**

## Why My Cat

Why my cat might be working for the...

Competition!!! (You know who I mean, the company down the road with the flashier sign, or who give their staff free tea and coffee, the baddies)

Due to COVID and lockdowns, like everyone else who has been able to work from home with a pet, they have found them to be "helpful"...

These "helpful" things my cat Rosie has done include:

Being cute and acting like she wants belly rubs. I keep falling for this trap

Glaring at me with a significant amount of disappointment being sat behind my laptop

Drinking the milk from my breakfast cereal bowl when I'm reading emails in the morning

Demanding to be let in and out even though there's a cat flap that she just used

Attacking cables because she's a cat

Deciding that my office chair is now hers as the 5 second rule applies

Going to sleep on my laptop case with the laptop in it and refusing to get off it

Wanting to sit on my lap when I'm trying to type

Thinking it would be a great time to climb over me as I'm trying to work

Demanding to be fed as I'm there and she is more important than anything work related

Vomiting up the food she's just eaten and then demanding more food

Joining Teams calls and showing other callers her err... yes... sorry about that

All of these take a little bit of time out of the day. So, you could say she's helping the competition, by trying to reduce my effectiveness of working from home.

But the greatest way Rosie has attempted to interfere with my working from home before yesterday was bring presents... If you have an outside cat, you know what I mean. If not ask someone with a cat and be prepared for some stories. Sometimes these presents are a little more alive and require catching and releasing. And there goes my tea break...

But yesterday she reached the pinnacle of cat lead diabolical interference. Directed at the office!!! Yes, you read that right, but fortunately I managed to intercept it and stop this evil operation, but it was close, very close. You might be wondering what could this 5 kg of fur, claws and cuteness could do?

Sometime overnight Rosie had turned a field mouse into a minion. I suspect Rosie then briefed this mouse on what to do (chew though cables I'm guessing) and placed this little field mouse in my shoe ready for her diabolical plan. As I ride a bike in to work, I put my shoes in my bag and head off. On arrival to the office at my desk I changed into my shoes and felt something strange... Very quickly I took my shoe off and looked in it and looking back at me was this little mouse, who seemed scared and shocked having just been squished further in the shoe by my foot. I'd manged to accidently disrupt Rosie's plan. After some initial surprise and keeping the mouse in my shoe I had to work out what next. Consulting with other team members it was decided as the mouse had definitely been coerced into this action by the evil Rosie Cat, that the most friendly course of action would be to release the mouse outside, giving it a new life living in the bushes in the carpark.

The culprit Rosie Cat, no one really knows what evil is behind that cuteness.

**Jamie**

# INCLUSION

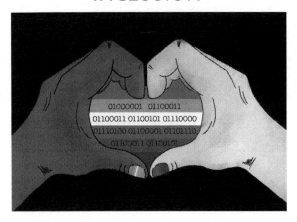

# Infusion

Inclusion is an infusion
a doing word of acceptance
making everyone stronger,
together, no more confusion.

Inclusion is everyone
no matter who you are,
or your background,
belonging because who
you are is truly valued.

Inclusion is where
everyone is welcome
and appreciated and
everyone has a part
in this beautiful blend.

Inclusion is being
somewhere you can
be your whole self
and be accepted for it.
Inclusion IS the solution.

**Collective Poem**

## Inclusion

Inclusion to me is...

Kindness

Respect

The way things should be

No-one left behind

Being non-judgemental

When people who are on the outside are seen, and "in" is
reshaped so that everyone can belong

Acceptance. Unwavering, unconditional acceptance of
what is before me. Be. Kind.

Acceptance of social divisions

About creating a kinder world with respect for all

The answer

Everyone, together

The right thing

Listening to someone without judgment, and then
putting yourself into their shoes

The obviously right and fair thing to do

Feeling like there's no "us" and "them", just "us"

**Collective Poem**

## Normal

Not odd

Or strange, but

Right in the

Middle.

Acceptable, accepted

Looking to fit in.

**Eleanor**

## Optimism

Blending into the crowd

in many ways but

with a smile,

a friendly face,

looking out to the horizon,

with curiosity

and optimism.

**Gail**

## Blank Canvas

A blank canvas,

waiting for the story

to be completed.

Incomplete but whole.

Seeing things eyes wide open

while waiting for lost souls.

Lips tightly shut

so as not to disappoint

with a smile to show

I am ok

but thoughts inside

that cause dismay

and challenge the painter

in every way.

**Jo**

## Acceptance

Not everyone sees you,

they may see a person

but not you.

Be yourself,

be true to who you are

and those that want to

will accept.

Be strong

and call on

those around you

as you take this road.

**Sheena**

## Accept

Accept yourself
  as you accept others,
Be curious
  and embrace their curiosity,
Smile and nod
  to show you are listening

**Eleanor**

## Learnt and Grown

In order to be accepted,

you must first accept yourself.

In order to accept yourself,

you must accept others.

For acceptance is taught,

It's learnt and it's grown,

it's human, it's kindness

and it stops us being alone.


**Jo**

## Normal

Normal

A word,

expectation,

acceptance,

or constraint.

A type of thing so many ain't!

Celebrate who you are

and make 'normal'

a word without power.

**Sheena**

## Smile

Smile, it will lift your spirits,

It will lift your confidence.

It will lift others' spirits

and make them want to join.

It won't always work but keep going.

You are as vital as they,

anyone who doesn't want to know,

more than they.

I would give this to my earlier selves,

not look at the floor,

afraid to make eye contact

in case someone laughed at me.

Finally, they laugh with me

(I think! And don't care otherwise anymore).

**Gail**

## Greater Reward

We

Deserve

Equity

Sad Frustration

You still don't get it

We are all born equal

Being constrained by your rules

We both suffer, we're both poorer

Setting me free brings greater reward.

**Lin**

# Us

Today we have been writing poems,

And thinking about inclusion.

We learned haiku and tanka,

Then cinquains and nonnets.

We worked alone and

Yet together;

Shared our thoughts,

And saw

Us.

**Ali**

## Wanted

The sky covers all,

No special favours, all here

Under the sky.

Belonging, safe, forever,

Seen and loved, you are wanted.

**Liz**

# Honeybees

See the honeybees,

They don't all do the same job,

But they're the same hive.

Working towards the same goal,

Together they are stronger.

**Laura**

## Between The Titles

Doctors and lawyers, accountants and bankers,
golf pros and artists and breakfast news anchors,
soul mates, just friends, the sad lonely hearts,
eligible bachelors (of liberal arts).


Students of Nietzsche and Jesus H. Christ,
the Stoics and Sophists, all equally spliced,
Those that love Kahlo, Picasso, and Pollock,
or see modern art as nothing but bolloc codswallop.


The sober and logical, the dour and stern,
the frivolous, ridiculous, the lacking concern,
the gamers, the readers, the realists and dreamers,
the 'tea with no sugar's, the 'coffee with creamer's.


The Cockneys, the Geordies, the Scousers, Manchunians,
Green Army, Red Devils, Beliebers and Whovians,
The pilots and dancers and poets and welders,
all meet at a church without any elders
without any sermons or speeches or prayers.
just a plain, musty room with old, comfy chairs,
to chatter and listen in equal measure,
about the enjoyment of life's simple pleasures,

Like hot baths and crushes and fig trees and kissing,

or finding that jumper you thought had gone missing,

like photos of parents before you existed,

or painting a room with friends you've enlisted,

bumblebees bobbing as though drunken on pollen,

and bright autumn leaves that've recently fallen,

or finding yourself a new favourite book,

and kids catching tadpoles in nets at the brook,

the pounding of raindrops drumming your tent,

surprise cancellations to dreaded events,

warm, salted butter and freshly baked bread,

a day without plans but staying in bed,

like giving yourself permission to cry,

like beautiful endings and perfect goodbyes.

They share all their stresses, anxieties, and fears,

like love lives and children and failing careers,

like going to parties they're scared to attend,

concern over money and how much they spend,

like elderly parents who're losing cognition,

and awaiting a call from the paediatrician,

and then they discuss the mistakes that they've made,

the friends that they've hurt and the trusts they've betrayed, and the more that their share, their secrets made known,

the more that they realise they're far from alone;

that despite all our differences, we are, above all,

no more than children, learning to crawl;

that life is a storm that's easier to weather,

when we focus on all that which binds us together;

and between all the titles by which we're defined,

the best's to be gentle, forgiving, and kind.

**Tim**

## All

Bird song is joyous.

They are many, together.

Doing their utmost.

Making delight of the day

Bringing union to All.

**Gail**

## Longing

Lying beneath the trees,

branches, leaves,

birds, bees, squirrels

and a breeze

I hear myself breathe.

This is peace.

Laying still

the butterflies decide to leave,

feeling now

what my body has been longing for.

**Mary**

# For The Silent Voices

*Page intentionally left blank*

## Unique Creation

The beauty of trees:

Strong, resilient, ancient,

Shelter, fuel, food, oxygen.

Every size, shape, colour,

Each a unique creation.


**Ali**

## Harmony

Busy bees are free,

Never once arguing for the

Colour of honey.

Busy bees work together,

In nature's harmony.

**Jay**

## New Dawn

Though unseen, unheard,

All life is carried forward,

Touched by a zephyr.


We share this breeze, each sailing,

Towards a shared bright new dawn.


**Jace**

## House Plant

Airy,

A splash of green,

A delight for the sight,

Watering them every week,

House plant.

**Charlotte**

## Squirrel

He comes,

Every day,

To feast on the bird seed,

And the birds don't seem to mind the

Squirrel

**Ali**

## Hedgehog

A wiggle

In the garden,

Making leaves shuffle, bugs jump

A home grower's delight, slugs and co. gone

A hedgehog!

**Gail**

## Home

The world

So large, and yet

When we are together

Able to stand as our full selves,

We're home.

**Laura**

## My Friend

Outrageously funny,

Terrible timekeeper however well-meaning,

Bold, brash, loving, loyal to the core,

She's the person I call in a crisis,

My friend.

**Mary**

## Friends

Standing

On the shoulders

Of giants and greatness

Of many fiercely beating hearts,

Friends.

**Liz**

## Raptor

Raptor.

Fiery devil.

Wait countdown to be free.

It hurts when you fly in only –

One line.

**Jay**

## Only If You Let It

My name is Kit and I have secondary breast cancer in my 30s. That means my breasts are literally killing me – my cancer started in my breasts and before it could be detected it had spread to my bones, lungs and even my skin. My cancer is incurable and terminal. I've been living with the disease now for just under 5 years that I know of, in reality I've probably had cancer for 6 or 7 years. When I was 33 I was told I'd be dead in under 6 months. That was nearly 5 years ago. I'm still going to die of cancer, I'm just doing it slowly!

You might be thinking "oh wow that sounds terrible" or "your life must be horrific". But that isn't the truth. When I was diagnosed I made a promise to myself to live my life and not just exist. I promised to see the joy in everything, even while my body slowly but steadily breaks down. One of the things I love most in the world is watching butterflies dance. They don't live for long, but they brighten the world and dance and spin as they move from one beautiful flower to another. That seems like a pretty good way of living to me.

People talk about battling cancer, but to me a battle implies both sides can win. I can't win. The day I was first told I had cancer was the day I was told I'd be dead in 6 months. In all honesty they doubted I'd last the week. But to me every single day that I wake up and see my husband is a day of victory. Every day that I get to do the job I love or visit an animal sanctuary is a win. I'm stealing back my life from cancer. My cancer can take my body, my health and even my life, but I refuse to let it take everything that makes me who I am today.

People often tell me how brave I am to deal with all of the side effects of cancer treatment. The truth is that I'm not brave, I'm just terrified out of my mind every single day. I really don't want to die a slow and painful death. But life didn't ask me what I want. I'm starting a new treatment next week in the form of IV chemotherapy. To administer the drugs to me, the nurse has to wear safety clothing, gloves and goggles because of how dangerous the drugs are. They will be put straight into my veins, right next to my heart! It isn't bravery that makes me go through with these treatments, it's fear of the alternative. Because the alternative is dying even sooner than I already am.

Other people seem to think that cancer has magically turned me into a wise woman. They want advice on how to live life to the fullest and how to keep smiling through adversity. My advice is simple. Life is too short for regrets. You never know what is coming round the corner. I was lifting massive weights in the gym 72 hours before I was lying paralysed in a hospital bed with terminal cancer. Hug the people you love. Visit that place you've always wanted to see. Most importantly of all, never ever regret getting older. It's a privilege denied to too many people. Life is a gift that you don't want to leave wrapped on a shelf. Life is the ultimate gift that keeps giving. But only if you let it.

**Kit**

# CHALLENGE

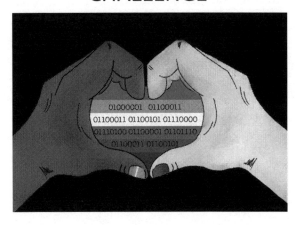

## My Challenge

My challenge is
to overcome obstacles,
to be my best self.
To be as kind to myself
as I try to be to others.
Simple things, like using
A toilet without having to
justify which one.

My challenge is to make
the most of everyday I can
and be thankful for what I have.
My challenge is trying to explain
why it's important to care about
the rights of LGBTQIA community
to people that don't care or understand.

My challenge is to recognise
that whilst I can do anything,
I cannot do everything.
And so, my challenge is
to love myself for who I am
And to try and do what I can.

**Collective Poem**

## Parrot To Panther

"I think I'm in the wrong room", said the

parrot to the panther.

"I wear a coat of many colours,

and yours is

but a coat of one.

How should we be together?"

The panther cocked

its head, curiously.

"Tell me of your colourful

coat, little parrot.

Which of your many colours

do you like the most?"

**Jamie**

## Timing

Rabbit: So, Tiger, I just had a thought. You seem very sleepy today, is it the heat?

Tiger: Rabbit, I am full, have had a hearty meal and now is a good time for a nap.

Rabbit: I see, that sounds like a good plan. Do you often have a nap?

Tiger: Why do you want to know? I don't need to think about it as I can catch food whenever I want and then sleep as nothing is going to trouble me.

Rabbit: I was just curious really as I wouldn't want to disturb you when you are sleeping.

Rabbit thought that he was doing so well and was incredibly frightened of Tiger. Tiger hadn't realised but Rabbit's tail was just under Tiger's paw as he had run so quickly trying to escape from a snake.
He kept chatting and could see Tiger's eyes start to close as he drifted off into a sleep.
Rabbit now took the opportunity to pull himself from

under Tiger's paw and run round to his back.
This had slightly disturbed Tiger, he woke back up and
as he did had the delight of Snake running into him and
Tiger finished his meal!

The moral of the story – timing is everything!

**Gail**

## Nature

I took a deep breath and patted my dog.

My dog jumped up and did a wee, on my knee, of all places.

He let out a cry and a passing bee said,

"Wow, that dog jumped high."

The dog replied, "Only because you stung my thigh.

Why, oh why, little bee did you do that to me?"

The bee replied, "Because I'm a bee, you see, and you

stepped on me!"

"It is in my nature, do you see?"

**Jay**

## Mongoose

I think I'm in the wrong room… said Mongoose as they surveyed a sea of serpents sipping water from great jugs, desperate to stay awake at the annual venom convention. The air was humid and the metal chairs, that were cold at first, were slowly being warmed by the midday heat, and the snakes were drifting off… when all of a sudden the door flung open, and a furry face peered around the corner. 'A mongoose', muttered Rattler, an older snake that had sat at the back anticipating a cheeky snooze. 'What on Earth, they are trying to make a mockery of us!' Some younger snakes also turned around, Mrs Boa furrowed her brow, 'He can be here can't he? I mean I'm not venomous myself but I always try to make these events to learn about my fellow reptiles…' She licked her lips, lunch time was still half an hour away. Mongoose audibly gulped, 'I'm trying to find the annual mongoose anti-venom research day? Am I on the wrong floor?'

**Rachel**

# Pelican

'So, I just had a thought…' the pelican started

As the group of animals around it all parted.

'Here we all are, disgruntled and starving,

While the furless turn our homes into tinder and kindling.'

'But why am I hungry and complaining right now?

When I have a veritable feast before me. So how,

About you all jump into my mouth, so I'll be well fed

And you need not worry about food or your bed?'

The capybara stepped forward, in front of the crowd

'I will go first.' They declared, unbowed.

The greedy pelican needed no further invite,

And opened their beak, to swallow in one bite.

**Jace**

## Worm

The worm wriggled out of the soggy soil,

created by the rain hours ago.

Greeted by the sun blaring down.

Meanwhile, the robin pecked at the ground

awaiting lunch to rise.

The squirrel darted past going for his stash.

A garden: thriving homes, plants,

And animals, for everyone to enjoy.

**Charlotte**

## Cost Of Victory

Covered in blood and soot,

Sen stood on the steps of the palace building,

staring down at the desolation

in the city below.

Clamour and battle rang out in the distance,

pockets of the old regime too afraid to

surrender or retreat.

'Victory…' he thought, bitterly.

'But at what cost?'

**Jace**

## Here And Gone

I think I'm in the wrong room,

or maybe the wrong me is here.

They look at me.

Through me.

Past me.

I'll be back soon, I say,

and break away for the rest of the day.

Or week.

Or month.

I return.

Thankfully, no one noticed I was gone.

**Jamie**

## Perfect Day

Going for a hill hike, there was much to see

and they ran as much as they could, with excitement,

as the day drew onwards.  They wanted to see the hills

across the valley and the sun glistening on the river.

They stood and looked across and saw what they hoped for.

They stopped there and gazed at the view

before heading back to their home.  It was a perfect day.

**Gail**

## Empty Can

'Wish you were here, Dad', I raised the can to my lips.

Strongbow, our cider of choice,

Necked in gardens and parks before heading home

Wiping our lips with a grin.

I guess this is still somewhere we could sit

As I emptied the can on the hard tombstone.

**Rachel**

# 6-word stories

Damn your closets. Life's my stage. **Jamie**

Here and queer, don't fear me. **Rachel**

He said. She said. Both me. **Jay**

Grandchildren? Again mum? Ask my brother. **Jamie**

At the beach; be back soon. **Gail**

'Dykes'! Hands dropped to our sides. **Rachel**

Mens Toilet. Womens Toilet. Gender Dysphoria. **Jay**

## Imagine

Imagine the default was both
Instead of this or that
Let me love both intensely
Arts AND science, dog AND cat

Or perhaps the default is either
I'll use whichever; go with the flow
You don't have to be sure and pick a side
Just freely hang out in 'I don't know'

If we weren't told over and over
that it's normal to be straight
Would you have tried on different hats
Has the patriarch decided your fate?

If the default was we all COULD like everyone
Some people would still pick a spot
It's a fluid spectrum of diverse combinations
You're either in love or you're not

Imagine the default was maybe
Maybe we're colleagues or Best Friends
Maybe you don't like people
Maybe love is something that bends

One size never fits all

It's maybe untrue that it even fits most

Loads of us hide, scared to be Other

Imagine the joy if the default was both

**Rachel**

## Flexibility

The room falls quiet, save for the hum of the electric light. I open my notepad to show that I'm listening. Curt surveys the ten of us. "Ok, people," he says, placing a hand on the table. "We've got a busy few weeks coming up, and we're going to need a few extra shifts from all of you. The business appreciates your flexibility." He's only the Deputy Head of Software, but since few of us have either met the Head of Software or read any of the marathon emails he circulates every Friday, what Curt says goes. "Any problems?" He adjusts the blood-red tie beneath his suit jacket.

Derek raises his hand, the one nestled in a black wrist brace. "I need longer to recover," he says. "I can't work long hours right now."

"You'll get time off in lieu. Recover afterwards."

Derek shakes his head.

"It's tricky for me too," I say, feeling all eyes fix upon me. "I can't do evenings or weekends. Childcare."

"Anyone else?" says Curt, his voice a keen blade.

\*

The scent of tomato, onion and freshly baked bread greets me as I step through the door. "Mummy," says a voice as a miniature yellow tractor bumps my foot.

"You're getting heavy young lady," I say as I lift Tara up. Two male hands grip my shoulders.

"You don't need this anymore," says Mark, removing my notepad from under my arm. He kisses my forehead and adjusts the name badge on his green overalls. "See you later."

*

"I'm not saying you're wrong, Aisha," says Grant. "I just feel like you could be better off working somewhere else." The office cafe smells of burnt coffee, sweat and ambition. Grant joined the company on the same day as me. He's in HR.

"Is that your professional opinion?" I ask.

"Not exactly," he says, laughing. "I just think that culturally… hey, actually, my friend Sanjay recruits developers. He'll be at my flat warming on Friday. Maybe you should come. You can be on my arm, if you like?"

I remove his hand from my shoulder.

*

"She's had another attack," says Mark.

"You didn't tell me," I say.

"She's OK. The doctor will call later. She's resting."

"Anything else?" I place my laptop on the dining room table.

"Her homework. If she's up to it. She wasn't earlier."

"I brought my computer home. I'm supposed to work."

He looks at his watch and frowns. "Sorry. I gotta go."

The front door closes, and the house is still. The last rays of dusk glint on the frame above the piano. My first class Masters certificate. The laptop chimes as I enter my password.

"Mummy?" says a voice in the lounge.

*

The ten of us are back in that meeting room again, and this time, there's excitement in the air. Curt grins at us with his straightened teeth. "We've had a standout month," he says, "and it's all because of you. Please accept these tokens of appreciation." With a few deft flicks of his wrist, envelopes skim across the table into hands and onto laps. "The business appreciates your flexibility. And your 'can do' attitudes."

Derek is staring at the closed door as he fiddles with his wrist brace. Only the two of us are empty-handed when the envelopes have been distributed.

*

"I have two more days of holiday," says Mark. "Two days. Until the new year."

"I know," I say, "it's just—"

There's a clatter on the staircase, and a small inverted yellow tractor comes to rest at the bottom.

\*

"I'm outside," I write in the app. A tick appears next to the message. Then another. Both ticks darken. I try to find his window in the apartment block as an icy breeze seeps through my coat.

"You came," says the reply. "Excellent. Be right down."

My breath escapes as a misty cloud. Behind me, the bus hisses, shifts into gear and pulls away, bearing its empty seats into the night.

**James**

# THIS IS ME

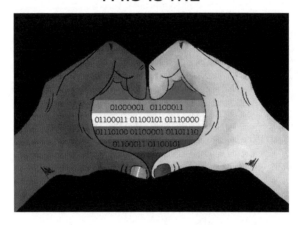

# I Am Still A Young Man

I was never a young boy

      And I never can be

I was a child

      Living with the burning certainty

      that I was somehow different

I was a young girl

      Relating only to my queer peers

      Only seeing boys at cadets

I was a teen

      Slowly figuring myself out

      Wanting to fit in as a lad with the lads

I was a young man

      Unable to relate to other young men

      Still surrounded by women

I am still a young man

      Despite still not being sure how to be

**Anonymous**

## No Limits

I am tired and in need of rest.

I am energised and full of ideas.

I am a confused seesaw.

I am not a fan of limits set for me.

I am going to rebel against them.

**Jamie**

# I Am

I am a data scientist

I am an artist

I am a nerd

I am a sister


I am an imposter

I am self loathing

I am conflicted

I am confused


**Anne**

## Umbrella

The umbrella that blew away,

Helping me to discover who I really am today,

Communicating, interacting & helping others,

they come naturally,

This catalyst guided me to make some little changes along

the way,

Believing in myself, building my own confidence each day.

**Michelle**

## Book

B eing transported to another dimension, place or time
whilst in the comfort of my own space;
O penly aware I have more books than I'll ever be able to
read;
O pen to new genres, characters, digital or paper back;
K eeping in mind that we don't all appreciate the same
topics, but are equally all connected to the pages of the
book.

**Charlotte**

## Safe

The river is calm,

It's peaceful, as I sit here

And I'm feeling safe.

**Elaine**

# Bend it Like Beckham

I can make that cheaper at home.
The words of a mum in distress,
The smile of a girl her name unknown,
   who has heard it all before but she just
wants to be on the field to impress.

Free from pressure, to play the beautiful game,
   but she must never forget or she'll get a lecture,
   she must learn to cook or she will bring shame,

Never forget, her roots, never forget,
   she can make it at home
   in her football boots.
In Wembley they roar her name.
She can make it at home
   for cheaper and with fame.

**Shaz**

## Sunshine

The clouds are fluffy
but no raindrops here to see
sunshine, feeling free

**Elaine**

## Clouds

Clouds are on their way,

Please don't stop too long today.

Sunnier times now,

Bring us better intentions,

Clouds to move on and leave calm.

**Gail**

## Trust

To one an oak,

May be overbearing.

But to all,

They are mighty, a sign of strength,

Trustworthy and overarching.

**Charlotte**

## Happy

Home and hearth,

A plan for my future, an idea,

Planting roots and finding my group,

Pacing forward, following my map.

Yesterday is gone, I'm living for today.

**Laura**

## Smile Glow

Smiling

More of my happy face

Is entering the world,

Like sunlight.

Enjoy the beams.


Go find less,

Let me be,

Outward happy,

Wondering free.


**Liz**

## Vulnerable

Valiant of being myself with humor, mostly improV

Under fire for standing proud, how about U?

Loving life though, keeping it reaL

Never giving iN

Expressing who I am, giving lovE

Ready to face the world, a little lighteR

And be all I can be, living my ideA

Because if I can do it, here's the ruB

Let me tell you, anyone can, because for reaL

Everything and anything is possiblE

**Jay**

# Sheffield

Steep hills that cars

Heave themselves up high

Even on foot you will breathe

Far more heavily, it's a faff

Fanning yourself on hot days feeling daft

Imagine never living anywhere flat, I

Envision myself becoming a fitter me

Loving myself more with every step till I fall

Down into the depths of the valley wood.

**Rachel**

## Unconventional

Unconventional, what a word, what a feeling.

Only one small step from weird or outcast,

one small sneer from alone.

Still, ever moving onwards, comfortable in my direction,

secure in those around me. Not too much, go find less.

This is me.

Spreading joy, sharing love, uplifting those around me.

Wholly myself, sister, daughter, friend.

Unconventional, what a word, what a feeling.

**Liz**

# In Front

We've all been there – scared, worried, afraid of what's in front of you;

Opening the door to a room filled with people, knowing you have to present for 1, 5, or 10 minutes at most;

Your eyes gaze around the room, easily spotting those around you for support;

Just 1 minute to go and it'll all be over –

strength, courage, remarkable, an achievement;

This is me.

I show bravery, commitment and loyalty to the task in hand and to others;

I give my all, not just for the presentation but for all involved including myself;

I give the best speech I believe I have ever given;

We've all been there – scared, worried, afraid of what's in front of you.

**Charlotte**

## Special Interest

I like to get into things,

especially interested in my special interest,

What if people get sick of me talking about it?

Excitedly sharing storylines from my favourite show,

Describing in detail the artwork I'm working on,

Singing along to every song on an album on repeat,

This is me. I love hearing others talk about their interests,

Making connections and spreading joy,

Letting others be themselves as I am myself.

My hobbies let me express myself the way I truly am,

I like to get into things,

especially interested in my special interest.

**Laura**

## Strength

Emotional - my greatest strength,

the ability to feel and empathise

Transported to other worlds

Daydreams where I feel connected to the whole of

humanity past and present

I feel everything,

the chaos, the destruction, death

Sometimes it gets too much

my brain won't stop whirring

then I'm on a rollercoaster that I can't get off

in a fairground that I can't escape from.

**Rachel**

## What People See

I am a transgender woman, that is what people see,

Do they see the heart, humour, or human, beating within me?

I love the buzz of friendly chatter,

I love cake and coffee with a natter.

I love discussing things that really don't matter.

This is me.

I give my ears, to listen, to thee

I give me heart, ever so gladly

I give my love, I give all of me

I am but one of many like me,

I am a transgender woman, that is what people see.


**Jay**

## Alopecia Awareness

I want to say something about Alopecia but I don't really know what to say. It's not my story to tell, it's my 7 year old daughter's. She has Alopecia Totalis and has lost all of the hair on her head. This is what I want to shout out to the world:

No, she doesn't have cancer – it's not caused through stress either.

No, there isn't a cure – well not one that wouldn't make her health worse.

No, we don't know whether she'll lose the rest of her body hair or whether anything will ever grow back.

Yes, it will make her more resilient, but damn it I wish at 7 she didn't have to be.

Yes, it's hard for me as mum, sometimes. I see the stares but she doesn't care she rocks her bald head when she's feeling confident. Stare away she's beautiful, isn't she?

She is more than her Alopecia, she is a mermaid, a singer, a budding mathematician.

A hilarious, sassy, frustrating 7 year old that will deal with it like a trooper.

Tell your story far and wide my girl and always shine bright, my little one.

**Anna**

## Love You Regardless

I've let you all in, so time to let my family in.

I have let my mum into my sexuality, something that has taken over 7 years and considerable emotional turmoil. It has felt like I've had to keep two isolated lives, one with my work/friends who I'm open with and the other life my family who don't know. Starting today, that wall has finally started to come down.

I chose not to come out, but to let my mum in to the fact that I'm gay. Letting someone in, a very subtle and different way to phrase it; a powerful way to open the door on my terms and waiting to see if they want to join me. What if the outcome is bad? It doesn't matter to me, my strength and who I am defines me, and that applies for when I let my other family members in (although, the reaction of my dad does scare me).

How did I come to this point? The support of my colleagues, my LGBTQ+ networks and a little comic known as Heartstopper. I am 33 and want to get on with my life now, I should not be scared of who I am and move forward with what I want to do next.

When I looked at my letting in message on WhatsApp, I saw a response from mum:

"I knew or highly suspected this and it doesn't and never

would have changed anything".

Years of worry and, such are mothers, she already knew and it didn't affect anything. She told me to keep being that voice for people that don't feel their beliefs are respected and who feel they can't be who they are.

This feeling is amazing and positive, because I felt pressure to come out for years which just didn't feel right. I literally skipped into work this morning with a beaming smile feeling that heavy weight off my shoulders.

"Thank you for telling me but it wasn't a surprise to me and I love you regardless"

**Radley**

# ALLYSHIP

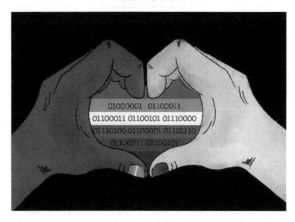

# Noise To Silence

Noise

Loud, Boisterous

Deafening, Earsplitting, Piercing

Clamor, Sounds… Hush, Quiet

Soothing, Calming, Relaxing

Peace, Tranquility

Silence

**Anonymous**

## Bully To Ally

bully

prejudiced insecure

judging commenting shaming

bigot hater friend supporter

learning undoing becoming

powerful changed

ally

**Claire**

# Allies

Acceptance, welcome
We are all here together
Each other's allies

**Kate**

## Cats

Can cats be allies?
Tiny furry supporters
No badges or pins

**Kate**

# Love

It smells like wet fur that comes from

happy splashing in puddles

It tastes like crisp winter air on a morning walk

It sounds like snores in front of the fire on a cold day

It feels like a cold wet nose snuffling for the

treats in your hands

It looks like 'who, me?' after leaving muddy paw prints

on a clean white floor

Love is a four-legged friend

**Claire**

# Rainbows

Rainbows

Curve gracefully

Encircling, protecting, holding

Red, yellow, pink, green

Following, flowing, shining

Refract spectral

Light

**Juliet**

## Support

Support

Unconditional, unwavering

Recognising, reacting, repeating

Solidarity, grief, anger, motivation

Co-ordinating, collaborating, commiserating

Focused, multiplied

Strength

**Amy**

## Together

Together.

Strong, Supportive.

Illuminating, Protecting, Loving.

I, They, She, He, We,

Saying. Acting. Understanding.

United. Visible.

Allied.

**Paul**

# Understanding

Understanding

Kind, Egoless

Evolving, Expanding, Opening

Knowledge, Links, Chains, Violence

Denying, Suppressing, Destroying

Judgemental, Decided

Prejudice

**Alyssa**

## Pride Allies

People of the world

Rejoice in who you are

In these (hopefully) enlightened

Days, we've come

Ever so far


A few years back

Life was not good

Living a lie was best –

In fear of an attack – but

EDI now makes life good

So things are being addressed


**Jackie**

## False Allies

Promote yourself as an ally. Promote yourself with boundless energy. Never lift others up.

Check all the boxes, running your race. Never look around to see who's alongside you, to see if the field is even, or its just your path that's clear. Meteoric. Of course you deserve it. Why wouldn't you?

So many words, so much face when you're visible, when it suits you to be seen. Surrounded by privilege, by your mirrors, you don't call out the voices that aren't there. Don't bring others in.

Proud of all you've delivered. When there's work to be done, where are you? Hard yards behind the scenes, organising, admin... so much privilege it's not just beneath you, it's beyond your understanding, your awareness. You're ready to walk on stage. What more is there?

'Something must be done!' A line on your plan. A title on the page. Yes, we must measure it. So important. Critical really. It's not for you to understand the roots, the systems, the processes. To draw out the experiences, the alternatives, to bring about the new. Another year. No change.

False allies. We see you. Do you see yourselves?

**Kate**

## Accomplice

accomplice

active, animated

collaborating, supporting, spotlighting

advocate, protestor, listener, learner

ignorant, unfamiliar, unaware

privileged, advantaged

majority

**Rosie**

# Support

```
                    SUPPORT
              RECEPTIVE  FLEXIBLE
            LISTEN   SPEAK   CARE
          HELP LOVE ATTACK   HATE
            GOSSIP   INSULT   HURT
            BIASED    PREJUDICED
                     JUDGE
```

**Jackie**

# People

Voice

clear, active

challenging, changing, championing

fear, misinformation, kindness, inclusion

supporting, lifting, encouraging

valid, worthy of respect

People

**Maura**

## Calm

It smells like pine needles

    in a mountain forest

It tastes like the last carefully chosen

    bite of an incredible dish

It sounds like waves crashing

    on hot sand at sunset

It feels like the chill of freezing air

    on your face

It looks like a snow-covered road

    with no-one for miles around

Calm is a moment in time,

    saved in your memory forever

**Amy**

## Joy

It smells like a wet dog
   who has been splashing in the stream
It tastes like ice cold soda
   on a hot summer's day
It sounds like raucous laughter,
   a joke you share
It feels like a tight hug,
   that lifts you up and spins you around
It looks like a smiling glance,
   meant only for you
Joy is living
   and loving

**Rosie**

## Love Is...

it smells like
    chocolate and roses
it tastes like
    hot cocoa on a winter evening
it sounds like
    fireworks
it feels like
    an old comfy sweater
it looks like
    a happy bubble
Love is
    hopeful

**Jackie**

# Exhaustion

Smells like
  an unwashed shirt
Tastes like
  the bitter acid of anxiety
Sounds like
  an empty house filled
  with echoes of daytime tv
Feels like
  enough is enough
  but never enough
Looks like
  a ghost going through
  the motions of life
All this,
  washed away
  by the smile of a friend

**Paul**

## Excitement

It smells like

a fizzing cocktail,

of citrus-sweet sugar

It tastes like

pink champagne

bursting candy bubbles

It sounds like whoops,

shouts and the slap of a high five

It feels like

a spring braced for joy

It looks like

a happy swig

from a spilling, clinking glass

Excitement

**Juliet**

## Anxiety

It smells like bleach,

stinging eyes

and burning your throat

It tastes like tar

being poured down your throat

It sounds like a shrill alarm

jolting you awake at 3am

It feels like being buried alive

It looks like crimson cheeks

and beads of sweat

rolling down a neck

Anxiety is debilitating

**Maura**

## Destroyed

It smells like charred ash
    that flakes away
    when I try to pick it up
It tastes like salty tears
    forming a well
    in my mouth
It sounds like fine glass
    shattering on a hard
    tiled floor
It feels like I will never
    be whole again
It looks like the ghost
    of a life once known
Heartbreak
    is the price of love

**Claire**

## Belonging

It smells like all our sweaty gear

in the back of a van

It tastes like too many cake sale cookies

and brownies and biscuits and cake

It sounds like so many mouths chanting

the same message that you can't make out

an individual voice

It feels like each hand being clasped firmly

with the reassurance of a trusted friend

It looks like a smile of recognition

as we pass in the hall

Belonging is the freedom to be yourself

and the safety to grow with others

**Alyssa**

## Unpredictable Love

It seems like a deep red rose
    opening in the morning sun.
It tastes like delectable chocolate
    melting in your mouth.
It sounds like birds chirping
    on a clear spring morning.
It feels like a comforting fire
    on a cold winter's night.
It looks like an ocean scene
    painted by God.
Love is unpredictable
    and love is breath-taking.

**Jay**

## The Unseen Wound

There is a scar you cannot see,
that runs the height and breadth of me,
and cuts me deep, right through my core,
and leaves me unlike me before.

There is a side of me that's hid,
that hides the things I saw and did,
that casts its unseen shadow wide,
and hides those parts of me inside.

There is a part of me so far
away from you, behind that scar,
that it's a country far away,
a foreign land from yesterday.

There is a part of me you miss,
the part of me before all this.
The part of me that I can share,
is all of me not still lost there.

There is a scar you do not know,

there is a scar I cannot show,

it bleeds in ways you cannot see,

and stains the unseen part of me.


When you go home, remember them and know;

for your today, they gave their tomorrow.


**Ben**

# ACCEPTANCE

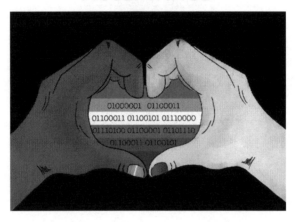

## Best Friend

You

Are Kind

Caring but

It's sad when you

Don't laugh at my jokes :(

You are an example

Of loyalty, accepting

Me for who I am, no judgment

Never too far away, my best friend

**Charlotte**

## Keeper

365 days of the turn of the Earth since you

Slipped in like fog on frosty mornings

Behind the furniture to disappear.

Wouldn't eat for seven days

Skinny as a whippet

We were worried sick.


365 days of the turn of the Earth you have

Learned to stalk as warrior queen.

Hide your baby shrews in boxes

Perfect untouched pink-brown commas.

You lurk on the compost

Wait for your next kill.


365 nights of the turn of the Earth you've seen

Fever dreams in the small hours.

Pressed your face to mine,

Ragdoll belly on my icy toes.

In sickness and health. Perhaps

You know us better than we know ourselves.

365 days of the turn of the world since you

Crept in and blew our hearts open.

Professional sleeper

Through fireball suns, Biblical rains.

The kids call to ask how you are. Perhaps

You know us better than we know ourselves.

**Lucy**

Keeper's Cat by Lucy

## 'bumbling in my head…

'it's all in your mind'

The pain

The clumsiness

The feeling 'different'

The longing to be like others...

The trying and failing

'you are just making excuses'


'I can see the problem'

The relief, the healing, the wholeness

Because in acknowledging brokenness I became whole

In accepting my difference, I received inner peace.


**Jane**

## Things I Can't Live Without

Love

Sense of worth

Sense of belonging

Self expression

Friends

And my cat. And gin. Chocolate...

**Sian**

## Vital Things

Things that I can't live without:

Not having to explain who I am

Knowing my partner and I are there for each other

Laughing and joking with friends

Listening to and playing music I love

Watching TV/movies that make me feel seen

Each feels as vital as the air I breathe

**Craig**

## My Church

Books and the libraries that house them
-        my church.
Spending time awkwardly writing
-        poetry and prose
Wandering around art galleries
-        with my partner pulling faces
Listening to music and dancing
-        at midnight
My community that makes up so much
-        of who I am.

**Rachel**

## These Are Things…

Things I can't live without
Getting lost in a book,
> invested in the characters
> and their storyline;
The sense of joy as I follow a team I love,
> watching them win and lose;
Laughing and joking
> until my cheeks ache;
Going for a coffee at a local café
> with my friends;
Being surrounded by loved ones
> near and far;
These are things that I can't live without.

**Charlotte**

## Things To Bring Me Joy

The daft and lovely face
      of my dog when she greets me
My partner's humour
      and fun-loving spirit
A good board game,
      well-competed
Being outside, for a walk,
      appreciating nature
Gossiping with friends
      like we don't have a care in the world
Sharing stories and learning
      about others' lives
These are the things that bring me joy

**Rosie**

## My Joyful Things

The freedom felt
>through movement and dance

Sweet treats
>in cake form

Love
>from family and friends

>enhanced by feeling human contact

The laughter
>brought by spontaneous moments

>that are sometimes fuelled by wine

These are the things that bring me joy

**Claire**

## Brighter Place

Water is a life keeper.

Breezes lift the fog.

Bird song is delightful.

Laughter lifts us all (that's science).

Dancing is just joyous.

Loved ones are the reason and always there.

And all make the world a brighter place.

**Gail**

## Things Of Me

My family and friends

Who make life fun

And give me

Purpose

Music,

Which feeds

My soul

My phone

Which connects me

And rules my life!

**Eleanor**

## My Things

Family and friends who make me smile,
reminiscing on past times,

Travelling around the world seeing other cultures,
foods and sights,

Music that makes me dance, sing out loud and soothing
relaxing tones

Running outdoors breathing in the fresh air and leaving
my troubles behind,

G&T (or wine) that crisp cold taste on a hot summer day
with friends!

**Chhaya**

## Things That Make My Heart Sing

Home or machine made,

     savoury or sweet,

     the act of eating is joyous.

A warm connection to those who care,

     cuddles hold me in my body

     whilst my spirit soars.

A song for every occasion,

     the backing track of my life.

An escape to my imagination,

     stories living other's experiences.

Crying, clutching, snorting

     laughter uplifts me.

The most powerful reason of all,

     love.

These are the things

     that make my heart sing.

**Liz**

# COMMUNITY

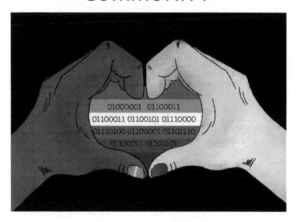

# Community

Community is a sense of belonging,

having other's back and knowing,

they have ours. It's looking out

for each other, not just now and then,

but all of the time. Community is family.

A group of people we surround ourselves

in a shared bond of trust. A safe space,

a safe place, safe in our diversity,

inclusive

like it always

should be.


Community is a beautiful thing.

Community is everything.

**Collective Poem**

## Biryani

Biryani, a food so complex I dare not make,

While it cooks the smell brings joy and takes you to your

youth, when you impatiently waited for that first bite,

It warms you inside with its perfect blend of spice and

makes you forget all your worldly thoughts,

It brings a noisy family to almost silence, it's a peaceful

Sunday dinner for all of 10 minutes.

**Shaz**

## Breeze

I see a whispered clearing amongst the trees, and through
a passing breeze
If only once I could be that breeze, if only momentarily
I could drift upon the wings of butterflies, around my life
with ease

**Jay**

## Happy Pride

Here I go, no missteP,

All around me, colour and glitteR.

Proud people no longer in need of an alibI,

Pacing through the streets as one crowD.

Years of hiding, now I can finally be mE.

**Laura**

## Things I Can't Live Without

Cake, that's fresh and baked for me.

Coffee, the way I like it, with a Miss or Mrs when served.

My kids who tell me about their day.

My community, of poetry, where I find my family.

Clothes, that fit, off the peg, I should be so lucky.

Hearts, which beat, with love, unconditionally.

Water, that sets me free, sustains me, and replenishes me.

Without these things, to be honest, I simply wouldn't be me.


**Jay**

## Arise

Droplets of rain
    break the surface
    of a pool,
    so deep and dark
    you cannot see its bottom.

How I wish
    I could plunge
    into its cool waters.

And arise refreshed
    and clear of thought.

**Eleanor**

## The Beach

The beach
  is the home
  of a million treasures.
I wish
  I could
  borrow it,
  and find a new wonder
  every day,
  tiny shells
  or stunning views.
And feel
  revitalised,
  curious,
  and in awe,
  all the time.

**Gail**

## My Life

The dense fog
   lifted to reveal
      a beautifully clear
        outlook.
If only
   I had that
      at my disposal.
It would make
   my life
      so much easier.

**Sian**

# The Escape

I look at the birds soaring overhead,
   and crave for their ability to fly,
   swooping and diving,
   having fun way up there;

If I could borrow their wings,
   I would take flight
   over the rolling green hills
   and valleys to the coast,
   lifted by the warm breeze,
   taking in all that lies beneath;

This is the escape I need,
   to get out and to feel free.

**Claire**

## Birds Sing

The birds sing
    their dawn chorus,
    greeting the new
    day's sun

I wish
    I could
    borrow them
    for darker times

To remind me
    that new days are coming,
    that the sun
    is on its way.

**Rosie**

## Moon

The waning moon
    that hangs suspended in dark,
    my mood shines through and captures it.

This netted moon
    I now use to convey my emotions
    simply by asking those to look up
    at the night sky.

And when the eclipse comes,
    they will know that I have
    simply chosen
    to no longer exist.

**Rachel**

## Great Oak

The great oak
   stands tall
   against all things,

I wish
   I could
   borrow its strength
   and stability

As I make my way
   forward through
   turbulent seas.

**Liz**

## The Sun

The sun shines down,
  unbothered by
  the people below,

I wish
  I could
  borrow its indifference

As I try
  not to let
  the world's emotions
  crush me.

**Liz**

## Wake Me Gently

The orange,
    yellowy hues,
    of the morning sun
    slowing creeping up
    beyond the clouds,

To borrow
    the soft light
    for each awakening,

To wake me
    gently
    with a smile.

**Chhaya**

# REFLECTIONS

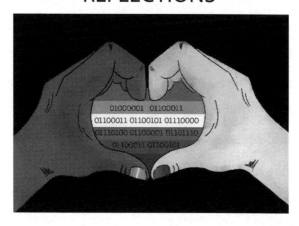

# Bean Sandwich

'Twas a cool day in September as the hazy afternoons of summer gave way to the sharp chills of autumn. Somewhere in an office not so very far away, an idea of malign design was about to be brought to the fore. A colleague whom I shall call NIGHT HAWK shared with those who were present an insight which might be described by some, and indeed by myself, as troubling. He informed us that sometimes he would take two slices of bread and fill them with cold beans. One might call this a bean sandwich, and one might recoil at the thought. The general response varied from slightly put off to outright shock that such a thing could be considered, let alone consumed on a semi regular basis. Feeling the issue had been fully scrutinised and closed, and with no desire to test this forbidden knowledge at home, topics of discussion moved on and thoughts of bean sandwiches passed out of thought and even memory.

However, as the evening rolled in, another colleague, whom shall be known as EAGLE GAZE, sent us an image with grave implication. A tin of beans in the fridge captioned "fancy a bean sarnie tomorrow?" I did not fancy this prospect at all, and could only hope and pray this was simply the delivery method for some humour, which in times such as these can be no bad thing.

Day dawned and there we were, at our desks, approaching what one might call 'snack time' when EAGLE GAZE decided to confess. She told us she felt the very urgent need to make and try this bean sandwich we had all been knocking, and in fact had brought one into the office to have as late breakfast! She pulled out a large mass of tin foil, and as my dread continued to build, began to unwrap it. What emerged was not just a bean sandwich, but a second-evolution bean sandwich, for this one had mayo, lettuce and red onion in it. It was a travesty. As the beans and mayo mixed into one viscous substance, it tested to the limit the structural integrity of the bread which contained it. Its very existence seemed to defy all natural order. All were unsettled by its presence, and even NIGHT HAWK looked concerned that the purity of beans and bread was corrupted by the mayo.

With no further ado, EAGLE GAZE went in for a large bite of the sandwich, having to manoeuvre in such a way as to stop the beany mass escaping into the office surroundings.

Some looked on in morbid fascination. I turned away, for I could not watch. NIGHT HAWK had a single tear in his eye, whether from the joy of vindication or despair at the addition of the mayo, it is impossible to say. All that I knew is that Pandora's Box had been opened, never again to be closed. After consuming a substantial amount of sandwich, though notably not all of it, EAGLE GAZE uttered a verdict to be etched upon the stone of human history.

"This is actually alright."

Make of this tale what you will, but I would warn you, if you are at home and see the bread and beans, and perhaps the voice in your head is telling you that heating up food is for the weak, remember what you read here and where the road leads.

The Bean Sandwich Incident is recalled solely by me and therefore the neutrality of the text may be disputed. Names of those involved have been hidden to mask their identity due to the controversial nature of the food choices involved.

**Sam**

## Ocean

The ocean

runs deep,

The fish

all swim

together,

The school

keeps them safe.

All manner

of fish

dwell here.

Infinity

diversity.

**Laura**

# Gloomy Days

Gloomy days ask for cosy nights in, curled up on the sofa
with a hot chocolate

Gloomy days mean staying in bed

Gloomy days call for battling the elements and cracking on
with things anyway

Gloomy days are for chats with friends to help bring a little
light in

Gloomy days entitle you to pause for a moment, just until
the sun says hello again

**Hannah**

# Drip

They feel the repetition.

They feel the tick of that clock.

They feel the reassurance of that certainty, the familiarity of pattern.

They feel the damp, the cold, the wet.

They feel the life it brings,

The green in the plants around us.

**Andrew**

# The Vixen

The indignant rooks who peck then cawing flap
From the burst and brokeback rabbit on the road;
The dipping ducks with naked feet,
Raw in the melt of the thawing brook;
The red kite soaring over the mumbling sheep;
Do they remember her?

Perhaps she eyed the smiling moon and laid down,
Breathing a long-last contented breath.
And wrapped in the womb-warmth of a remembered den
Saw again the goldening light of summer's last sun
As her pups yelped and yawned.

Hard against the hedge-thorn, a stiff white brush,
And ice-furred flanks in life full red.
The prick-eared compass of her head pointing forever west.
Not – like the rabbit – snatched;
But gently, kindly taken up by the frost.

Do you think to see her ghost
Run across the gorse-marked heath,
To see her quick and lithe again?

I won't look to see her but

I hope for many mornings

When stream-sound, hill-view

Wood-smoke, life blood,

Leaf-mold, dung and death

Capture eternity.

**Mat**

## Fog

For some, fog is a muddle

    – it's gloom and grey and hides the light


For others, fog is the calm

    – it's waves of cool and a barrier to unwanted spotlighting


For many, fog is the prelude to clarity

    – it's an opportunity to take stock under cover and make
a plan of action


**Roseanne**

# Rain

rain brings blossom
   in the spring

rain brings the hope of rainbows
   to the hopeful mind

rain brings chatter
   to the office

rain brings coats
   out of the wardrobe

rain brings summer to an end
   it is a reminder of the cycle of life

**Ana**

# WRITING EXERCISE

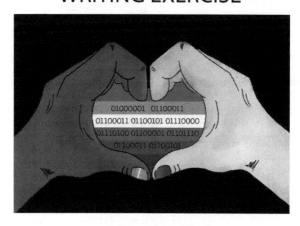

If you have ever thought of writing a poem, but are not sure where to start, try this exercise and feel free to adapt it in whatever way works for you. Don't be surprised if the poem you create is different from what you had in mind at the outset.

**Haiku Writing Exercise**

A Haiku is a short, three-line poem, exploring the external world (often as a metaphor). It has three lines of 17 syllables. Line 1 and 3 have five syllables, line 2 has seven syllables. Take something in nature that could be used as a metaphor. If you want a stretch then associate the second line, with human life, and the last one a lesson we might learn.

*For example*

**busy bees are free**

**never once arguing for the**

**colour of honey**

*Your Haiku does not have to rhyme*

# INDEX

# DIVERSE VOICES 2022

*"Acceptance" by Jamie-Lee*

First published in the United Kingdom in 2022.
©Diverse Voices
Each poet has asserted their right under the Copyright,
Designs and Patents Act, 1988 to be identified as the
author of their work.

First published in the United Kingdom in 2022
by Bite Poetry Press.

First Edition

ISBN 978-1-915787-17-0

Cover image: "Acceptance" by Jamie-Lee

Design by Gerard Winter-Hughes
Printed and bound in the UK by Biddles, Castle House East
Winch Road, King's Lynn PE32 1SF